ALPINE GLOW

Studies in Austrian Literature, Culture, and Thought

Translation Series

Peter Turrini

ALPINE GLOW

Translated by

Richard Dixon

ARIADNE PRESS

Ariadne Press would like to express its appreciation to the Austrian
Cultural Institute, New York and the Austrian Ministry of Education
and Art, Vienna for assistance in publishing this book.

Translated from the German *Alpenglühen*
©Thomas Sessler Verlag, Vienna, Munich

Performance rights remain with Thomas Sessler Verlag

Library of Congress Cataloging-in-Publication Data

Turrini, Peter.
    [Alpenglühen. English]
    Alpine glow / Peter Turrini ; translated by Richard Dixon.
        p.   cm. -- (Studies in Austrian literature, culture,
and thought. Translation series)
        ISBN 0-929497-95-3
        I. Dixon, Richard S., 1953- I. Title. II. Series
    PT2682.U7A7813   1994
    832'.914--dc20
                                        94-16234
                                        CIP

Cover design:
Art Director: George McGinnis
Designer & Illustrator: Paul D. Rodriguez

Dramatis Personae

The players in this story:

THE BLIND MAN, about 70 years old.
JASMINE, about 50 years old.
THE BOY, about 20 years old.
A TYROLEAN MOUNTAIN GUIDE
20 SINGING TOURISTS (unseen).

Scene 1.

(The stage is dark; absolutely nothing can be seen. Dark and still. After awhile the spectator's eye begins to get used to the darkness on the stage and only then starts to recognize lines of contour. A person lies in the middle of the stage, on the floor, unmoving and naked. Scattered pieces of clothing lie about him. A bed stands at left, at the foot of the stage; beside the bed there is a suitcase, or, perhaps, an overnight bag. Nothing moves; all is quite still. The stage lightens gradually (or is it only, perhaps, that the viewers' eyes have gotten used to the darkness?). The nude at the center of the stage is a thin old man, fully turned in on himself. Another person lies on the bed at the foot of the stage; yet the figure remains unidentifiable: it is completely covered over by a blanket. The bed is an old camping cot.

A ray of light, the vanguard of the rising sun, falls across the stage. The naked old man raises his head slowly; he listens, touches his uncovered head, then suddenly aware of his nakedness, he gathers up the scattered pieces of clothing. He retrieves glasses with dark lenses, puts them on, and dresses sitting up: first, the long underwear, shirt, pants; then tie, jacket and, lastly, shoes. This process continues while the sun rises higher in the sky.

The audience of this play witnesses a mountain sunrise of such beauty that it could only occur in popular sentimental movies or on the pages of tour-

1

ist brochures. Light from the rising sun falls into the porch, through the glass front which stretches across the entire expanse of the rear stage screen. Massive mountains tower up behind this glass front, and, between two of these peaks, the blood-red sun rises ever higher.

Nothing decorates the wall of the porch room except for a large mirror, a Tyrolean hat and an oil lamp. Doors open into the room from left and right; these lead, apparently, to other rooms. The porch room, the few pieces of furniture which grace it, and the old man's suit as well, give the impression as if they all came from another time—perhaps the late forties or early fifties.

Finally, the old man is dressed; he stands. He looks over to the camp cot, where the figure, still covered, lies motionless. He holds his head slightly askew and smiles. He moves, his hands stretched out a bit, slowly toward a door. He opens the door and disappears into an adjoining room. The figure on the camp cot turns and groans in his sleep. One sees locks of red hair. The old man returns to stage with a tin pail filled with water; he also carries several tools. He puts down the pail of water, takes a toothpaste tube and squeezes toothpaste into his mouth. He brushes his teeth. Next, he shaves, using a shaving brush, shaving soap and razor. He cools his face with a shaving stone, in the same way men cooled their faces years ago. He takes the Tyrolean hat from its hook on the wall, positions himself approximately one meter from the edge of the mirror, not in

2

front of the mirror, but, indeed, next to it. The man looks intently at the wall and adjusts his hat. It takes a few minutes before he is satisfied with the way the hat looks. He turns towards the glass front of the porch room. The sun is now higher in the sky and the room is so illuminated from its light that the old man, who stands now with his back to the audience and squints into the sun, appears to be some kind of supernatural, luminescent apparition. He stretches out his arms as if he were embracing the new day; then, he lets his arms fall to his side, turns around, takes off his hat, returns it to its hook on the wall, goes to the middle of the room, stops, tilts his head and looks out into the audience. Silence.)

BLIND MAN (*with a smile*): Dark and quiet, as usual.

(The blind man stands and looks into the audience. Nothing happens. The blind man listens. A young farm laborer enters the porch room from one of the doors at right. The boy carries in his hand a basket with eating utensils. He puts it down. The boy goes over to the blind man, stands next to him and looks out into the audience. Silence.)

BLIND MAN: So, what's new in the world?

BOY: Everyone's happy; the people live in peace. Men go about their daily work with joy and good will.

BLIND MAN: That's nice.

(The boy lays his head onto the blind man's shoulder. The blind man caresses the boy's head. There is something mechanical to the whole action, as if it were an automatic and daily occurance. Silence.)

BLIND MAN: I have something nice to report as well. Someone has come. A young woman.

(The blind man points toward the camp cot. The boy goes to the cot and contemplates the locks of red hair. He raises the blanket. An undistinguished woman, fifty or so, wrapped in a tiger-fur coat, comes into view. She has deep red hair and looks, as far as one can tell, rather unkempt and worn-out. She is still sleeping and does not move. The boy stares down at her.)

BLIND MAN: Do you remember a few weeks ago when I gave you a letter to mail? It was a letter to the Society for the Blind. For forty years, I wrote, I have been sending in my dues—always on time—and for forty years I haven't asked one thing in return. And what, from the very beginning, when I joined, right up to today has been offered? Maybe it was a kind of bouquet, dried flowers, picked at the height of their beauty by the gentle hands of small children . . . dried especially for its members and offered at Christmas time as a modest but comforting greeting. Or, like today, a drastically reduced price on an inexpensive stay at the Harmony Home for the Blind, where every

4

room and every corner shows a seldom seen consideration for the needs of the sightless. And so the Society has cared for—and continues to care for—its valued members. It spoils them with small and great indulgences, offers them discount rates of any and every kind. Still, I really didn't care for the dried flowers then, and I'm not interested in any vacation rate at the Harmony Home today, either. And why should I take away from another blind comrade, that which I already have around me in such bounty here? What do I need with dried flowers when flowers of every sort grow and flourish right before my door? Or why should I move into the Harmony Home when I have lived in harmony up here for almost fifty years? The only thing I ask, as I wrote in my letter to the Society for the Blind, is for them to send me up a woman, a young, attractive person, who loves, as I do, the great classics of literature. A student, maybe, with whom spirited discussion would be possible, who would match word for word, and for whom the arrangement might be as stimulating as for me, until, perhaps, other things might develop between us, more passionate and intense. And last night that wished-for person, that young woman arrived. Tired from the long trip out and steep climb, she went to bed without a word, and I lay down beside her so that I would lose not a moment of her newly won presence.

(The boy touches—with a mixture of astonishment and curiousity—the woman's shoulder. The woman does not move. The boy shakes her. First, softly; then more harshly. While the blind man speaks, not moving from his position, the boy goes into a side-room and returns with a small table. He takes the groceries from the basket and places them on the table. He prepares a kind of breakfast.)

BLIND MAN: This morning there are good reasons to remember another morning. It was the morning of the first of September, 1939. During those late summer days, my classmates and I lingered in Italy; we lived in a small Pension along a bay inlet in the Gulf of Sorrento. The day began and, with it, the usual late summer heat, which always drove my friends to the beach early. I ate breakfast and stayed behind a bit, on the balcony. Then I went down to the beach, to the bathhouse. It wasn't the sea's deep blue which had captured me then, but the word, l'amore, love, which had been painted across the wall of the bathhouse with red paint in an unsteady hand. Long drops of paint ran down from every letter of that word; they had dried in an uneven pattern along the wood clapboarding. Who was it who had announced his love here so awkwardly, yet so dramatically, to the waiting

6

world? An old fisherman, perhaps, grown stingy with his words and his emotions, with one word only for his beloved wife, after so many midnight expeditions had kept them apart? Or was it the work of his wife? Did this sole word express the anguish of one left behind, the entire pain of loneliness in one small, mute word; or, was this, instead, a sign of exultation, scrawled in an instant of frenzied joy? For which unknown beauty was this word on fire meant?

(The boy watches the woman and the blind man. The woman does not move.)

BLIND MAN: Oppressed by the glut of these thoughts, I closed my eyes—my eyes could still see back then—and I imagined what the woman I would love some day would look like. For a long time, I couldn't see anything—just blackness. Then, slowly, a figure formed out of the darkness: a young girl in a white dress with two large pockets sewn to the sides. The girl had reddish blond hair; she moved toward me and smiled. And at that moment, I heard my friend shouting that the war had broken out, but I didn't want to open my eyes because this girl, who was still just an image, was not meant to fade away, not at that moment.

(The blind man tilts his head and smiles. The boy

7

stands next to the blind man and, likewise, tilts his head.)

2.

(Silence. The boy stands next to the blind man. Both tilt their heads. A jet airplane leaves behind its trail of condensation across the blue sky in the background. Silence. The red-haired woman in the fur coat stretches and rolls back and forth on the cot.)

BLIND MAN: Tell her that I am ready for the official welcome.

(The boy moves to the camp cot. He shakes the woman. She pushes away his hand and sleeps on. Silence. The boy upsets the cot. The woman falls to the floor. Beneath her fur coat she is wearing a sickly green dress. She looks up. Her face is pale and swollen. She tries to orientate herself. She opens her luggage and takes from it a bottle of pills and a bottle of whisky. She washes down a handfull of pill with a swallow of whisky. She searches in her luggage, throwing out several objects in the process (rubber penises, condom packages, etc.), until she finds a particular object: an old paperback edition of William Shakespeare's Romeo and Juliet. *She smoothes her hair back with her hands, sits, legs extended, on the floor and looks up at the blind man. She opens the book, removes a bookmark, and be-*

gins to read the part of Juliet.)

WOMAN (*to the blind man*):

> Wilt thou be gone? It is not yet near day.
> It was the nightingale, and not the lark,
> That pierced the fearful hollow of thine ear;
> Nightly she sings on yond pomegranate tree.
> Believe me, love, it was the nightingale.

BLIND MAN (*answering in her direction*):

> It was the lark, the herald of the morn,
> No nightingale. Look, love, what envious streaks
> Do lace the severing clouds in yonder east.
> Night's candles are burnt out, and jocund day
> Stands tiptoe on the misty mountain tops.
> I must be gone and live, or stay and die.

(*The woman speaks the part of Juliet, the blind man Romeo. He knows his lines by heart; she reads from her book half-heartedly until, at one point, she loses her place and cannot find it again.*)

WOMAN:

> Yond light is not daylight, I know it, I.
> It is some meteor that the sun exhaled
> To be to thee this night a torchbearer
> And light thee on thy way to Mantua.

(*Finally, she gives up and looks at the blind man.*

She feels ill. She tries to stand up, but cannot manage it.)

WOMAN: (*to the blind man*): Do you have a name? What's your name, anyway? Oh well, it doesn't matter. What's a name anyway? Whenever a John comes to me and wants to tell me his name, I tell him, keep your name to yourself. To me, you're Claus or Herman or Gerald or whatever else I want it to be. And whenever he tells me that his little wife, the missus whatever, doesn't like it in the ass, you know what I mean, doncha, then I tell him how to give it to Erika, or whatever her name is, so that she will like it. Oh God, I've lost my place. That's always a problem with me. My name is Jasmine, with an "e"—Jasmine, it's a French name. That has its advantages and disadvantages. The advantage is that I get more Johns because they all think I'm French. Some think, though, that I do French style automatically, without a surcharge; and, so I guess that's one of the disadvantages as well. "French" isn't included in my basic price. It's extra, part of my deluxe service. The young girls just starting out do everything for the same price, but they do it 'cause they're dumb and just can't wait to start earning their living; you know, travel, see the world and all that. I'm getting off the subject again. The Society for the Blind

10

gave me two thousand Schillings plus travel expenses and they told me I should act like a lady 'cause you've got culture and, anyway, you're old and blind. So I thought, give the poor dog a break and go get your old school books. And, so you see, I found this play there, too. Hey, do they have this in braille?

(*Silence.*)

JASMINE: I mean, since you seem to know it by heart already.

BLIND MAN: When I became blind forty years ago, the only things you could get in braille were the classics. Then, they got "The Best from Reader's Digest." I read all the classics, most of all the love scenes, over and over. It's a well-known fact: almost all love scenes end tragically, most of the time, fatally. So why, given all this catastrophe, should I still yearn for love? And so I sought solace, even though in vain. My loneliness grew, and my desire for female companionship grew even more.

(*Jasmine tries to stand up. She struggles; finally, she stands. She leans against the wall. Silence. Jasmine regards the blind man and the farm boy.*)

JASMINE: (*to the boy*): Who's he?

(*Silence. The boy stands next to the blind man.*)

JASMINE: (*to the blind man*): I've got a suggestion as to how we can do this. Everything's paid already, and as long as I seem half-way attractive to you and you think it's okay, then we can go ahead and do it right away. Then I can catch a ride back into town.

(*Silence.*)

BLIND MAN: I can't see you.

JASMINE: What? Oh, yeah. You'll have to excuse me, I've done a lot of things in my life, but I've never done it with a blind man before. I mean, there were plenty who wore glasses, even ones with tunnel vision—you know, they can only see a little bit of what we see. We see a clock tower, but all they can see is the clock; you know, stuff like that. But you're the first one who's really blind.

(*Silence.*)

BLIND MAN: Would you do me a favor? Could you go over to the mirror and describe yourself to me?

(*Silence. Jasmine glares at the blind man. She moves slowly toward the mirror and looks at her reflection. She looks at herself in all her ugliness. She begins to laugh out loud. The laughing stops. Silence.*)

BLIND MAN: You are very beautiful, aren't you? I

knew that you were beautiful. You have a white dress on, don't you?

(*Jasmine looks at herself in the mirror one more time, then looks at the blind man. She moves to the overturned camp cot, sets it aright, and returns the scattered objects to her luggage. She sits on the edge of the camp cot, sniffs and looks at the blind man and farm boy.*)

JASMINE: You know, it's against my principles, but here I go with these charity cases. I guess I have a soft spot for cripples.

(*Silence. The blind man and the boy look at her. The blind man opens the case of his braille watch and moves his hand over the face.*)

3.

(*The blind man touches the face of his braille watch.*)

BLIND MAN: It's about time for the rooster.

(*Deftly, the blind man opens the window of the porch room. He sticks his head out of the open window and imitates the crowing of a rooster.*)

BLIND MAN: Nature, too, has its order and its precision.

(He closes the window of the porch room; he closes the cover of his braille watch as well.)

4.

(He closes the cover of his braille watch. Silence. Neither the blind man nor the boy make a move. Jasmine stands, takes the boy by the hand and leads him to the camp cot. She rummages through her overnight bag, pulling out a couple packages of condoms.)

JASMINE: You're one of those who doesn't need one of these. I can see with my own eyes that you're a mama's boy. You just want to please. If you don't understand anything about psychology in this business, you might as well forget it.

(While she speaks, Jasmine removes her stockings.)

JASMINE: Anyone can spread her legs, but to be able to say in a second what kind of john you got—that takes years, maybe decades of experience.

(She caresses the boy's head and pushes him down gently toward her naked feet.)

JASMINE: He's a good boy. He's a good boy. If you know his type well, there's nothing more you need to do. He does it all himself.

(*She leans back and begins to eat. Silence.*)

BLIND MAN: What's going on here?

JASMINE: Breakfast is being eaten.

(*While the blind man speaks, the boy raises up his head slowly.*)

BLIND MAN: My dear Jasmine, this is the first time that I've called you by your name. I'd like to tell you that I don't misjudge this moment. I am an old man, and I suffer from a handicap which, despite all the progress of modern science and especially the more advanced experiments of National Socialist doctors is no longer treatable, all the admonishments of the monthly Aid to the Blind journal articles to the contrary notwithstanding. You are a rather young woman; life lies before you. And, all things considered, I realize quite well, even if the long hours of loneliness have led me to confuse a sentence or two here and there, that I am still coherent when I tell you, and tell you straight out—I want you. I am not a poor man. Since the governmental policy establishing equal claims for military and non-military injuries, I have accumulated, through my pension, a rather large sum of money. My activity here in the mountains has added further to these funds in not an insubstantial manner. In the event of my death, this money would, naturally, be

15

transferred to you. If you would but turn your face toward me and allow your heart to make one sacred vow, you might take into consideration all these things I have told you.

(*The sky above the mountain peaks becomes cloudy. Jasmine eats and drinks. The boy places his head between his legs.*)

BLIND MAN: I know that this is a lonely place and that a young person needs other people and other diversions. I've thought a lot about that. And in this house, which seems so isolated from the rest of the world; there's not even electricity, but there is a radio—vintage 1956 model, runs on batteries, which need replacing at the moment (I ordered new ones a long time ago). The batteries should've been here long ago; I can't imagine what has happened to them, and sometimes I think that this boy, normally a dependable and trustworthy helper, has, for some unknown reason, kept the batteries from me so that I have no idea what's happening in the world and am completely dependent on him for any such information. My dependence on him for any news gives him some kind of strange delight; and I can't help but notice the satisfaction he takes from this and, have thereby discovered one of the darker sides of that young man's personality. He's capable of anything,

16

and some of it not very positive, if you ask me, just like the other people who live up here in these mountains. They're a strange lot, private to the extreme, suspicious and prone to fits of fury—the farther up you go, the worse it gets. The farm where this fellow comes from, one of the highest in the area, is just a stone's throw from here, you know. There've been plenty of times in the past thirty years when I've been left without batteries for the radio. And if it isn't the boy to blame, then it's the post office itself and their lousy service. Between 1962 and 1964, I didn't have any batteries at all; those years are a total blank for me—I don't know what went on in the world then. My health, apart from an occassional toothache, is tolerable; still, if you should so wish, I would be willing to leave my present domicile here in the mountains for short periods, and accompany you to the nearest village so that we could seal our relationship legally. It would also be a good opportunity, perhaps, to take advantage of the recent offer from the health department for a free and complete physical.

(*Jasmine pushes the boy to one side.*)

JASMINE: You want to get married?

(*Jasmine stands, moves toward the blind man and leads him to the camp cot. She pushes him gently*)

17

down onto the cot. The boy runs out of the room. Jasmine takes a mail-order catalogue from her luggage and sits down next to the blind man. The boy looks in from outside, through a window. Jasmine leafs through the catalogue.)

JASMINE: The most important thing is to find a wedding dress. White might be a bit too much, but pink would be all right. This model is 100% viscous. Order number L 58 0225. Elegant design, top with pointed clasp. Sizes 38, 40, 42, 44, 46 and special orders. The fur coat, which I'm wearing, is from this catalogue, too. 40% modacryl, 40% polyacryl, 20% polyester. You stay in fashion; trendy with a collared scarf, hooked clasp. Very snuggly.

BLIND MAN: Very nice.

JASMINE: What else do you need for a wedding? A cuisinart which can put it all together. Let's see . . . Order number L 30 3891. It kneads, mixes, beats, chops, cuts, dices, squeezes, has a mixer attachment, herb-dicer, lemon squeezer, juice press and puree attachment, too.

BLIND MAN: Wonderful.

(Jasmine looks at the blind man. The blind man looks at her, not at the catalogue.)

JASMINE: You know, sometimes I get the feeling that you blind guys aren't really blind at all.

18

(*Jasmine leafs through the catalogue.*)

JASMINE: Wedding service, "Seventh Heaven." 79 pieces: 6 soup dishes, 6 dinner plates, 6 dessert plates. 6 cups with saucers. 24 piece silverware, 6 beer glasses, 6 wine glasses, plus a 7 piece serving set. With 12 place mats. A one-time, sale price of 898.00 schillings. With guarantee against breakage.

BLIND MAN: Unbelievable.

(*She looks up. The blind man looks at her. She closes the catalogue and puts it aside.*)

JASMINE: A wedding with a blind man doesn't really make any sense, really, when you think about how things look. Maybe that makes it all the more beautiful on the inside. Stand up.

(*The blind man stands. He positions himself next to the camp cot with his back to the audience. Jasmine stands and kneels before the blind man. She begins to perform manual sex. The blind man uncovers her. The boy's face disappears from the window. The audience can see Jasmine's hand moving back and forth.*)

JASMINE (*after awhile*): You know, when a person stumbles onto a case like you, where things don't go smoothly at first, you gotta ask yourself, what are you doing all this for? Why do you knock your head against a brick wall, year in and year out? Why don't you

19

just let things go and get out of the business? And, do you know the answer? You do it all for the kids. My eight-year-old son goes to a school where he learns to speak French. From first grade on they learn the language. And do you know how much it costs to send him to a school like that? My youngest one, the three-and-a-half-year-old, she goes to a private kindergarten. You can't send them to public school anymore, it's filled with foreigners. My oldest goes to the school for hotel management in Feldkirch. He's almost done. With a diploma from that place, he can walk right into any job at any four star hotel in the country . . . or three star one, anyway.

BLIND MAN: Why don't you stop what you're doing, Jasmine dear, I've got something I must tell you. I believe that, at the beginning of any intimate relationship, one should always be open and honest. That's why I need to tell you that, after forty years of sustained isolation, I have no feeling at all down there anymore.

(*Immediately, Jasmine pulls her hand away.*)

BLIND MAN: Of course, it was as a consequence of my blindness that I had to learn to know the world through an intensified sense of touch. So, if I feel anything at all, it is through my fingers.

JASMINE: You've given me a bit of a shock for the moment. But you'll see how well I can adapt to circumstances; it's a professional requirement, you know. Put out your hands; spread your fingers.

(*The blind man does as she tells him. He holds his arms outstretched, spreading his fingers. Jasmine retrieves a packet of condoms from her bag and rolls two over the blind man's index fingers. Silence.*)

JASMINE: What do you say now? Can you feel something?

(*Silence. The blind man moves his fingers quite slowly.*)

BLIND MAN: May I tell you the story of how I lost my sight?

(*While the blind man speaks, Jasmine puts her stockings back on. She takes her shoes in one hand, her luggage in the other, and moves very slowly, on tip toes, toward the door.*)

BLIND MAN: I wanted to become a journalist and see the world in all its glory. I wasn't going to let one bit of it escape me. I was hungry for news and stories, newspapers and magazines. I studied journalism at the University of Vienna, only then it wasn't called journalism as such; that came later. In 1952 I got a chance to go to America on scholarship along with some West-German students. Three months after I got there I was

21

asked by my professor if I wanted to witness an atomic bomb test blast in the ocean. Naturally, I said yes. We were taken out to the South Sea site near the island of Elugelab on an aircraft carrier. The press officer led us into a kind of armored room and asked us to wait first for the blast and only afterwards to look through the peephole. I was just too curious to wait and watched the whole thing from beginning to end. It was just like in the newsreels, only that the mushroom cloud wasn't black, it had many colors to it. Elugelab island disappeared, of course, beneath the blast. Later on, the press officer distributed sea shells to us as a kind of souvenir from Elugelab. This is mine.

(He takes a sea shell from his coat pocket, searches for Jasmine with his hands, then gives her the shell. Jasmine stands next to the door. She seems greatly changed. Silence. The blind man opens the cover of his braille watch.)

5.

(He opens the cover of this braille watch and feels for the time.)

BLIND MAN: Oh my God! I'm late with the cuckoo.

(He moves to the glass front, opens a window, sticks out his head and imitates a cuckoo bird. He closes the window, then counts.)

BLIND MAN: Twenty-one, twenty-one, twenty-one, twenty-one, twenty-one, twenty-one.

(He opens another window and again imitates a cuckoo, this time with a somewhat higher voice. He closes the window; he closes the cover of his braille watch.)

6.

(He closes the cover of his braille watch.)

BLIND MAN: In the beginning things were okay. I didn't have the slightest problem with my eyes. Then, after a little while, I noticed that I couldn't see as well as I used to.

(Jasmine stands at the door; she is not sure whether she should go or not.)

BLIND MAN: The doctors talked about some kind of lack of oxygen supply to the optic nerve. I'll spare you all of the technical stuff about the attempted surgery, its failure, et cetera. My parents, wealthy business people from Graz, bought me this house in the mountains. They said that the mountain air would slow down my progressive blindness, at least for a little while. Today that kind of idea seems ridiculous, doesn't it? But, back then, that's what we wanted to hear—so that we wouldn't be engulfed by a sense of total helplessness, so that we wouldn't be forced to prepare for the worst. Total blindness came one morning. I woke up, opened my eyes; but it was still night. And it seemed an eternity, probably only a minute or two, before I grasped the fact that I was blind, that this night around me was, for everyone else, bright daylight.

(*Silence. He moves his fingers. Jasmine watches him. She takes a jar of make-up, the kind theater actors use, and a role of toilet paper from her luggage. She wipes off her make-up. Without make-up, she appears much differently than before.*)

BLIND MAN: I regarded the world in a way made possible by my blindness. In a short time I learned braille. I read the classics, which may have led to the fact that since then I have adopted a sometimes rather theatrical way of expressing myself. I subscribed to the "Best from Reader's Digest" as soon as it was possible to do so. In 1956 I got my first battery-operated radio. Immediately, after that, that's all I did. I listened to the radio night and day; I used up batteries right and left. I imagined the events of every news broadcast; I painted my own pictures of what went on. For example, I would imagine a train wreck: first the train, then the countryside around it, then the people in the wreck. I imagined them lying about on the ground, bloody and dying; then the arrival of the ambulances. And when the picture was done, I put in the colors. The deep green of the fields and trees; the bright red on the ambulances. Naturally, a train wreck in England would have different colors to it than one in, say, north Africa. I have lived in this house for forty years, but that doesn't mean I have retreated from world affairs by any means. Quite the opposite, in fact; I've taken in everything the world has had to offer—albeit on my own, rather limited, terms.

(*Silence. The blind man moves his fingers. The cloud cover over the mountains becomes now quite thick. Jasmine removes her fur coat. She takes some pieces of clothing out of her luggage and puts them on. First, a wool vest, then, a winter anorak. She seems totally transformed. She puts the fur coat in her luggage, places the sea shell gently on the floor, puts on her shoes and gets ready to leave.*)

BLIND MAN: In 1957 the first satellite orbited the world. It was called Sputnik I; I was thrilled!

(*Silence. Jasmine stops at the door.*)

BLIND MAN: (*in an increasingly louder voice*): And then Fidel Castro took over Havana; I was happy about that. And when they built the Berlin Wall I tried to imagine how they could build a wall that went through an entire city and how the people, friends and families were split up . . . that made me unhappy. In between all this there were the usual events, you know, airplane crashes, fashion shows, terrorists in the south Tyrol. Then, suddenly, they landed a man on the moon; I was beside myself with excitement. But the workers' unrest in Poland got me worried, but at the same time gave me a glimmer of hope. And the new car models came out in Zurich and I imagined all the hoopla at the showroom, you know. . . .

(The blind man begins to shout.)

BLIND MAN: . . . But I couldn't imagine it because my mind was still in Saigon; all I could see was those Vietnamese children. All I could imagine was the color of their wounds. And then another war broke out—the Yom-Kippur War—and then another and another. I just couldn't keep up with these things . . . I couldn't picture them fast enough. I kept losing the details, the color. First, the color went; there just wasn't enough time to put in the color. I saw things in black and white. And, after a few years, I didn't see anything at all. I listen to the news, but it doesn't mean anything to me anymore. I couldn't even imagine German reunification . . . and I couldn't care less if socialism lives or dies. Sorrow and joy don't exist anymore; they've disappeared. I don't see anything anymore, I'm just afraid, horribly afraid. I haven't listened to the radio for months. And the truth is: I told the boy not to bring anymore batteries into the house. But tonight . . . what a miracle has happened! Tonight, as I lay beside your bed, suddenly I saw the image of that child who fell down a mine shaft three years ago. Don't you remember, they had to dig a second shaft just to get to him. And this morning, before you woke up, I saw that word again, the same word I saw in 1939 painted on that old bathhouse. In red paint.

(*Silence. The blind man moves his fingers. He tilts his head and smiles. Jasmine is visibly nervous.*)

BLIND MAN: Are the condoms on my fingers colored ones?

JASMINE (*uncertain*) : I'm sorry? Oh, no.

BLIND MAN: Do they have colored ones?

JASMINE: Yes, I think they do.

BLIND MAN: Do you have some?

(*Silence.*)

BLIND MAN: Please.

(*Silence. Jasmine opens her luggage and searches. She pulls out several packs of condoms. She goes over to the blind man and places colored ones over the blind man's fingers. The blind man moves his fingers.*)

BLIND MAN: What colors are these?

JASMINE: Blue.

BLIND MAN: Can I really believe you?

(*Jasmine nods her head. Long silence.*)

JASMINE: Yes.

BLIND MAN (*happily*): I've got a blue finger.

(*The blind man moves another finger.*)

BLIND MAN: And these, what colors are these?

JASMINE: Red.

BLIND MAN (*happier yet*): Now I have a red finger.

(*Jasmine names the colors of all ten condoms.*)

JASMINE: Red. White, in other words, flesh tone. Violet. Green. Red. Flesh tone. Yellow. Black, silk. Red. Blue.

BLIND MAN (*in total joy*): First, I have three red fingers. Then, two flesh tones. I have a green and a violet finger. A yellow one, a blue one and even one in black silk.

(*He laughs.*)

JASMINE (*despairing*): Please, stop it. I have something I need to tell you. I am not the kind of person you take me for. I work in the main office of the Society for the Blind. They gave me your letter to answer. I was just pretending all this; I played a cruel trick on you.

(*The clouds in the background now cover the sun. It grows darker in the room. Silence. She takes off her red wig. Her hair is already somewhat graying; it is tied back in a bun.*)

JASMINE: There is no excuse for my behavior.

(*Silence. She takes his hand and places it on her head. Silence.*)

BLIND MAN (*good-humoredly*): May I take a guess at the color of your hair? Reddish-blond?

(*She looks at him. She does not answer. Silence.*)

BLIND MAN: I've guessed correctly, haven't I? And your dress? May I take a guess?

(*He is becoming ever more gleeful.*)

BLIND MAN: It's white, isn't it?

JASMINE: Yes.

BLIND MAN: You're wearing earrings, too, aren't you? They're jeweled. It's . . .

JASMINE: Yes, yes.

BLIND MAN: Aquamarine. Blue aguamarine. They hang down from your ear, silver and blue. Under your right ear. Silver and blue. Both stones are aquamarine.

JASMINE: Of course.

BLIND MAN: And your figure? Excuse me, but I mean, what does your figure look like?

(*Silence. The blind man turns toward Jasmine; he tilts his head. He is very happy.*)

BLIND MAN: I'd say, rather slim . . . am I right? Particularly slender around the waist.

JASMINE: Very trim.

BLIND MAN: I can see it! My imagination works again! I can see just what you look like!

(*Jasmine begins to cry.*)

BLIND MAN: And the weather? Is the sun shining? No, let me tell you: the sun is shining. And the whole room is bright with sunlight! And in the middle of all this brilliance—you!

(*Jasmine takes her bag and runs from the room. The blind man notices this immediately. Silence.*)

7.

(*Silence. The blind man rips the condoms from his fingers. He tilts his head and listens. Silence. A very long silence. The blind man kneels and touches the floor, as if, by doing this, he were to find Jasmine again.*)

8.

(The boy enters. He holds a birdcage in his hand; a small rooster with bright feathers sits in the cage. The blind man crawls over to him. He touches the boy, recognizing him immediately. He continues to touch him, as if he cannot accept the fact that the boy is not Jasmine. He feels the cage.)

BLIND MAN: What's this?

BOY: My favorite rooster.

BLIND MAN: And what are you going to do with it?

BOY: Give it to the lady.

(The rooster crows. The blind man stands up and laughs.)

BLIND MAN: Twenty years. No, thirty years. No, forty years. For forty years I've been waiting for a woman like that. I've tried to fill the time by memorizing great love scenes and saying them out loud. I've tried to banish my need for a woman by burying it with news and current events. But, it always comes back. Out of the darkness. The shape of that woman takes form, the form comes out to me and awakens everything I have tried to hide, cover or bury. And when I go to embrace her, she vanishes. Her colors. Her contours. They dissolve back into the darkness. Tonight she came back from the dark-

31

ness. She didn't dissolve away. She stayed. It was no dream, no memory called up from the past. She was real. A flesh-and-blood woman. In a pretty white dress. She had a wonderful figure, too. And reddish blond hair. She wore silver earrings with aquamarine stones. And she knows the great love scenes as well; at least, one of them. And this unbelieveably beautiful woman, blessed both inwardly and outwardly—this . . . Helen of Troy . . . —she's supposed to be thrilled by the idiotic present of a rooster from some alpine fool like you? A barnyard rooster? What do you want to give her that for? What's going on here? You're not allowed to give her anything. No one in your family is allowed to give her anything. You don't have anything left that's worth a damn to give. You've already given it all away—to strangers, foreigners—tourists! Your time, your land, your soul! The only thing left for people like you is to serve. You've become a race of lackeys. You're mountain lackeys, that's all you are. Mountain lackeys. Mountain lackeys.

(The blind man is completely winded. He leans against the wall and breathes heavily. The boy sits on the cage and buries his head in his hands. Silence. The clouds in the background separate slowly. Silence. The boy listens. The rooster crows. The blind man imitates the crowing of the rooster.

Silence. The blind man listens.)

BLIND MAN: Gone. She's not coming back.

(*He goes to the boy and leads him to the glass front. He stands next to the boy.*)

BLIND MAN: So, what's new in the world?

(*The boy is silent. The blind man grabs the boy by the neck.*)

BLIND MAN (*full of bitterness, almost hate*): I said, so what's new down there? I want to hear you say it!

BOY (*in a monotone, as if by heart*): Everyone's happy; the people live in peace. Men go about their daily work with joy and good will.

BLIND MAN: That's nice.

(*The blind man presses the boy's head to his own shoulder. He caresses the boy's head. The boy tries to work loose, but the blind man holds his head firmly. The boy frees himself forcefully.*)

BOY: The whole land is burning up! The animals are burning up! And the flames are burning holes in the sky!

BLIND MAN: What kind of nonsense is that?

BOY: Everything's on fire. It's out of control!

BLIND MAN: Idiot.

(*The boy goes over to the oil lamp. He takes it from

the wall; takes the rooster out of the cage, pours the kerosene over the rooster and ignites it. He throws the burning, screaming animal at the blind man.)

BLIND MAN (*shouts*): Help! Help! Stop it! Stop it!

(The boy takes the burning rooster and places it in a trash can filled with water. The sound of the fire extinguished by the water is heard. Smoke comes up out of the trash can.)

BOY: But it can't be stopped, can it?

(Silence. Far away, a group of about twenty people is heard. They are singing.* They sing an Austrian mountain folksong. the singing approaches slowly. The clouds in the background dissolve. Jasmine enters. She puts her luggage near the door.)

*(Translator's note: The group depicted here sings with German accents. This suggests foreign, i.e. German, tourists climbing about Austrian mountains, and thus reiterates the blind man's tirade at the boy several lines previously.)

34

9.

(She moves back and forth within the room, talking and talking, and paying no attention to the singing outside, which gets nearer, and, hence, louder and louder.)

JASMINE: I'm sorry that I ran away like that without any explanation. Please, listen to me. You were very honest with me. The story of how you lost your sight moved me a great deal. I would like to try to be as honest and open with you and the boy now. I would like to tell you who I am and what possessed me to seek you out dressed in my disgusting disguise. I grew up in the country and was raised in a very religious family. My mother used to tell me that I had some kind of guardian angel, who was always with me. As long as you stay a child of God, she would say, your guardian angel will protect you and keep you from harm. It has been the great tragedy of my life that what she used to tell me was true. My guardian angel not only kept harm away from me, it kept everything away. As long as I can remember, people have been confiding in me, telling me their sorrows, their joys. They tell me everything, while I have nothing to tell them. My life is a blank. For twenty years I have worked in the main office of the Society for the Blind. I answer the letters our members send in, I take care of whatever problems they might have with laws or whatever. I give them advice; I comfort them. Sometimes I even play matchmaker for two sets of weak eyes who, under normal circumstances, would never have seen the path to their beloved. I can tell when two people are made for each other. But when I see a pair that I've brought together walking hand-in-hand down a hallway at the Home for the Blind, I always think to myself: so, who will take *your* hand? Where is the one who is made for you? Where is *your* destiny? You've got two strong, healthy eyes; you see perfectly, yet nothing ever happens to you. The blind all around can't see a thing, yet their lives are filled with beauty and happiness. I envy them; sometimes I even hate them a little. Please, don't misunderstand me, blind people are wonderful people. Why, I know a young man who was blind from birth. He studied hard and now he's some kind of translator. He has unemployed actresses read poems and novels onto tape and then he translates what they've read into another language. He, a blind man, makes literature come alive for people who can see. And when I asked him how he came to terms with his fate, he said he loved his life, even though there was pain he could not get rid of. For example, he could never throw devastating glances to women he desired. Isn't that a wonderful answer? No man has ever bothered to throw a devastating glance my way. I love children more than anything, but no man has ever told me that he wants me to be the mother of his children. And when I sit in the park and see how some parents abuse their children, I want to walk up, take away their children and raise them myself. I would keep them far away from anything ugly or loud. On vacations we would go to an exercise farm in southern Styria, just so that we could lose weight together. I'd pay people money not to give me food. The massages there are wonderful, but you've got to pay extra for them. I just can't afford to pay for as many as I would like. Sure, I've had a couple of boyfriends before. The first one lasted about one night, the second one hung on for a couple of weeks until I saw him one night with another woman. He forgot to break up with me. That's when I decided to settle for something more permanent. I wrote to the prison for sex offenders. If there's anyone in your institution, I wrote, who is about my age, very lonely and would like a long-term personal relationship, then I would be willing to help out. Yes, indeed, there was one individual—in for life—a former official at the State Ministry. He was sent to the prison for cutting off a prostitute's breast and carrying it around in his briefcase for days. He might be a possibility. I wasn't shocked at all. I can understand almost anything, even if I can't forgive it. Anyway, I was intrigued and so, I went. A small, good-looking man sat in the visitors waiting room; he was the murderer. I only visited him three times. His life had been as empty as mine, and whenever we talked about his crime, he found it as grotesque as I did. Actually, we agreed on almost everything, and by the third visit, we didn't have much more to talk about. So, I stood up, said goodbye as politely as I could and left before visiting hours were over. Then I got your letter. The loneliness you described reminded me of my own. But the question was how should I approach you? I'm not a young girl anymore, you know. Should I just show up as I really am? You wouldn't even have given me a second look; until today, no one gave me a second look. So I thought up a disguise that was different from anything I had ever done in my life. I read books about prostitution. I visited the streets where prostitiues hung out, and I watched them ply their trade. The more I got involved in the project, the more exciting my life became. I've always been able to adjust my personality to fit the need. I had decided to be a whore; I wanted to get rid of my guardian angel, I wanted to get rid of him forever. I wanted to be your whore and experience everything whores experience . . . (*she screams*) What is that!?

10.

JASMINE: What is that!?

(*Jasmine stands before the trash can; the legs of the drowned rooster stick out of the trash can. She pulls the half-burned rooster out of the trash can and regards it incredulously. The blind man and the boy stand next to each other and look toward Jasmine. Outside the loud singing of the Austrian mountain folk song dies away. The last stanza, then: silence. A Tyrolean mountain guide enters. Jasmine is so surprised by this course of events that she continues to hold onto the rooster throughout the scene.*)

TYROLEAN (*in an aggressive tone, to the blind man*): The tourists just marched right by your window! And another thing: you were five minutes late with the cuckoo!

(*The blind man moves to the glass front, opens two shutters. Outside, the weather is beautiful. The blind man speaks to the tourists underneath the window.*)

BLIND MAN: Ladies and Gentlemen! By now you have a few hours of hard climbing behind you. I am sure one or two of you toyed with the idea of giving up, of simply stopping in your tracks, sitting down and letting the others go on without you. But, you got over that thought and thus gained an important victory over your own worst instincts. Your reward lies before you. The Austrian Alps offer you the most breathtaking of any alpine view you could ever imagine.

If you will, turn your eyes, your cameras, your walking sticks toward the distant peaks on your left. This is the 3501 meter high Highpoint. Next to it the famous Jacob's Peak. 2741 meters high. Now let me tell you briefly how that mountain got its name. Once there was a certain fellow named Jacob Geiginger. During the last century Geiginger wanted to declare his love to his beloved so strongly that he climbed the peak to shout his devotion to the people below, one of whom, coincidentally, was the young lady herself. Since that time, the peak has been known as Jacob's Peak. And, whether or not, after a few years of married life, our friend Jacob climbed back up the mountain to shout out declarations of, shall we say, a less passionate, kind—well, the chronicles are silent on that topic! Next to Jacob's Peak is the Sugar Cap, 3507 meters high. Below, at the foot of the Sugar Cap, you can just see the jackdaws circling about. And, if you can't see them, at least you can hear them!

40

(The blind man moves away from the window and gives a couple of short, shrill screams. He is imitating mountain jackdaws. Then, he turns again to the window to continue his talk.)

BLIND MAN: Here, as you see, nature still reigns supreme. Flora and Fauna exist side by side, unspoiled. In these woods the playful muskrat lives in peace beside the timid mountain deer. Here the gentle hummingbird shares the sky with the proud eagle. Here the faithful Crossbeak flies with the vain turtle dove. Next to Sugar Cap Peak you can see Timmel's Yoke, 2470 meters high; and, next to that, the Wilderness Peak, with its 3772 meter high altitude probably the highest and most impressive mountain of the entire chain. Regard this proud mountain in all its majesty. If you look carefully, you'll be able to discern something moving through the bush. Perhaps it's a ram or a sturdy mountain buck.

(Again, he bends away from the window, gives several quick whistles. He imitates the cry of a ram. He goes to the window again to speak to the unseen tourists.)

BLIND MAN: To the right of Wilderness Peak, the White Cap towers over all. Although to the naked eye both peaks seem equal in height, there is a difference. Look closely. White Cap is fully 43 meters lower than the Wilderness Peak. Next to White Cap, the peak to the extreme right is known as the Bell Tower: 3358 meters high. This mountain has been preserved appropriately as one of the last refuges for our buzzards. You can hardly see it, however, as it lies a bit too far off in the distance. Therefore, close your eyes and concentrate; listen to the buzzard's call.

(The blind man moves away from the window, takes a leaf of grass from the inside pocket of his jacket and uses it to imitate the call of a buzzard. A long drawn-out tone is heard. The tourists below the window applaud. The blind man repeats the imitation a few times until he becomes red in the face. The Tyrolean guide closes the window and disdainfully gives the blind man a couple of bank notes.)

TYROLEAN: Better make that cuckoo sing on time or I'm docking your pay.

(The Tyrolean leaves the room swiftly.)

11.

(The Tyrolean guide exits. The blind man goes, still holding the bank notes, into a side room. Once again, the Austrian mountain folk song echoes across the stage. It dies away slowly. Jasmine is still holding the charred remains of the rooster. The

blind man re-enters the room. Silence.)

BLIND MAN: What are you holding in your hand, Jasmine? The rooster? He's dead, isn't he?

(*Jasmine drops the rooster back into the trash can.*)

BLIND MAN: He was the boy's favorite pet. He wanted to give you the rooster as a gift. When I enlightened him as to your profession; when I told him what kind of perverse human being you were, that you did it with everyone, that you were a piece of meat for sale, that your genitalia resembled a barn door, through which a whole company of filthy men have marched in and out . . . in and out . . . , and that you could be paid to do anything. . . . after I told him all this, he went crazy and set his favorite pet on fire right in front of my eyes . . . or rather, my nose.

(*Silence. Jasmine looks at the boy and smiles coyly. The boy returns her smile.*)

BLIND MAN: What's going on here?

(*Silence.*)

BLIND MAN: Jasmine, take a closer look at this piece of raw nature. He's of limited intelligence, prone to fits of anger. Low forehead, ape-like. He has no depth, no background. He takes everything just as it comes. He can't even conceive of the fact that behind a whore there often lurks a saint. He understands nothing of metamorphosis, of interpretative skills or the powers of imitation. He doesn't understand a thing about theater.

(*Silence. Jasmine and the boy smile coyly at one another.*)

BLIND MAN: What are you two up to?

(*Silence.*)

BLIND MAN: A few years ago, when he came up here to bring me some food for which his greedy father always overcharged, this boy couldn't utter two words back to back. He couldn't say a thing. I taught him how to speak. I had to literally train him how to speak. He never could learn more than one sentence at a time.

(*Silence. Jasmine and the boy still smile at each other. With a dexterity that is quite unexpected, the blind man grabs the boy by the scruff of the neck.*)

BLIND MAN: So what's new in the world? What's new in the world?

(*The boy defends himself.*)

BLIND MAN: What is new in the world?

BOY (*mechanically*): Everyone's happy; the people live in peace. Men go about their daily work with joy and good will.

BLIND MAN: That's nice.

(*The blind man tries to press the boy's head onto his shoulder and caress him. The boy resists, runs away, goes to Jasmine. He leans his head on her shoulder. Jasmine caresses him. She takes him by the hand; goes with him to the door. She looks once more at the blind man, takes up her luggage and leaves the room with the boy in tow.*)

12.

(*Jasmine and the boy leave the room. Silence. Through the glass front of the porch room, the audience can see the two stop in front of the house. Jasmine speaks to the boy. The boy exits. Jasmine returns to the house. The sky darkens, as usual in the mountains, in an instant. The blind man crawls around on the floor, touching everything as if he could find the two through touch.*)

BLIND MAN (*screams*): Don't leave me alone! Don't leave me alone!

(*The blind man touches the trash can and pulls out the burned rooster. He imitates the rooster's crowing.*)

BLIND MAN: I do imitations! I imitate the sounds of dead animals! The Chamber of Commerce pays me to do it!

(He imitates a large rooster. He imitates a cuckoo. He imitates a mountain jackdaw. He imitates a ram. He imitates a buzzard. Silence. Jasmine enters. She now wears her hair, which had been tied back in a bun, undone and free. She has removed her shoes and wears an unbuttoned jacket over her green dress. Her appearance has changed dramatically. She places her luggage carefully to the side and stands quite still. The blind man senses that she is in the room.)

BLIND MAN: I do imitations. I imitate a lonely and deserted man.

(He sobs. Silence.)

BLIND MAN: I imitate a blind man's destiny.

(Silence. He imitates his own voice.)

BLIND MAN: I studied journalism at the University in Vienna. Only then it wasn't called journalism as such; that came later.

(Silence. He screams.)

BLIND MAN: I never studied journalism. I hate reporters.

(Silence. Jasmine watches him; she does not move.)

BLIND MAN: And I don't have the slightest idea whether the island of Elugelab even exists or not, or whether it ever existed. The story about the atomic test blast I got from Reader's Digest.

(*Silence.*)

BLIND MAN: The sea shell belongs to some stranger. He came to the mountains after vacationing on Mallorca.

(*Silence.*)

BLIND MAN: I was a die-hard Nazi.

(*Silence.*)

BLIND MAN: I tried to sabotage the telephone by blowing up the lines.

(*Silence.*)

BLIND MAN: The plan literally blew up in my face.

(*Silence.*)

BLIND MAN: Not at first, really, over the course of a few years.

(*Silence.*)

BLIND MAN: Some friends brought me to this house in 1945, until my de-nazification process could be completed.

(*Silence.*)

BLIND MAN: I was never really a Nazi.

(*Silence.*)

BLIND MAN: I was just doing an imitation of a Nazi.

(*Silence.*)

BLIND MAN: I do imitations.

(*Silence.*)

BLIND MAN: I can imitate the way a blind man
walks.

(*He imitates, in an exagerrated manner, his own
gait.*)

BLIND MAN: I can imitate the way a blind man
holds his head.

(*He tilts his head sharply. Silence.*)

BLIND MAN: Maybe even my blindness is just an
imitation, too?

(*Silence. Jasmine looks at him intently. A long
pause. The blind man moves his hands slowly toward his glasses as if he intends to remove them. At
the last moment he stops. He smiles.*)

BLIND MAN: Dark and quiet, as usual.

(*Silence.*)

JASMINE (*to the blind man*):

> Wilt thou be gone? It is not yet near day.
> It was the nightingale, and not the lark,
> That pierced the fearful hollow of thine ear;
> Nightly she sings on yond pomegranate tree.
> Believe me, love, it was the nightingale.

(*Jasmine takes the part of Juliet; she recites by
heart, without using her paperback. She plays Juliet with beauty and grace. The blind man answers*

her, likewise without use of a book, by heart. He plays the part with less pathos than before.)

(The two play the scene to its conclusion.)

BLIND MAN:

It was the lark, the herald of the morn,
No nightingale. Look, love, what envious
streaks
Do lace the severing clouds in yonder east.
Night's candles are burnt out, and jocund
Stands tiptoe on the misty mountain tops.
I must be gone and live, or stay and die.

JASMINE:

Yond light is not daylight, I know it, I.
It is some meteor that the sun exhaled
To be to thee this night a torchbearer
And light thee on thy way to Mantua.
Therefore stay yet. Thou need'st not be gone.

BLIND MAN:

Let me be ta'en; let me be put to death.
I am content, so thou wilt have it so.
I'll say yon gray is not the morning's eye;
. . . I have more care to stay than will to go.
Come, death, and welcome! Juliet wills it so.
How is't, my soul? Let's talk. It is not day.

JASMINE:

> It is, it is. Hie hence, begone, away!
> It is the lark that sings so out of tune,
> Straining harsh discords and upoleasing
> sharps.
> Some say the lark makes sweet division;
> This doth not so, for she divideth us.
> . . . Since arm from arm that voice doth us af-
> fray,
> Hunting thee hence with hun's up to the day.
> O, now begone! More light and light it grows.

BLIND MAN:

> More light and light, more dark and dark
> our woes!

(*Long silence.*)

JASMINE: You knew? From the very beginning?

BLIND MAN: What is it that I am supposed to have known about?

JASMINE: That I am really an actress?

(*The sky above the mountains darkens again. The first drops of rain begin to fall against the glass panes.*)

JASMINE: I love when it gets like this. Let's sit down.

(*She pushes the camp cot in front of the glass front. She takes him by the hand, leads him to the cot and pushes him gently onto the bed. She takes matches from her luggage, goes over to the oil lamp, raises the glass and lights the wick. She lowers the glass and adjusts the flame. She sits down next to the blind man.)*

JASMINE: It's really beautiful here. It's one of my favorite times of the day, now, between late afternoon and early evening. Sometimes I pull down the blinds in my apartment as early as noon just to create the same mood. Then, I stretch out on the couch and practice Juliet's lines. Actually, I practice them every day. For thirty years—day in, day out. And just because I've never said them on stage, does that make me less of an actress? I've had three abortions. An acting career and children don't go together. My first boyfriend wanted to be an actor, too. We took the entrance exam for acting school together. They took him, but not me. So I tried private acting lessons. My boyfriend was too superficial; he had no depth to him. We split up. Art and artists need time, sometimes years. I tried everything. I got the addresses of all the theaters from the almanacs, and I wrote a letter to every one; I sent photos, too. Only a few bothered to write back. Whenever I was invited to read, I went immediately. I always got there way too early. I checked into a cheap hotel and waited for days until it was time for my au-

51

dition. I always started with Juliet, what else? At first, they listened patiently, and asked me whether I had any other role I had prepared. No, I said, I didn't. I didn't want any other role. It was this or nothing. Later on, they would interrupt me after the first line or so. They didn't understand that this character doesn't have a thing to do with age. This character lives through the soul of the artist and it doesn't matter what that artist looks like. Juliet is inside of me; why couldn't they understand that? They sat in their little theaters; they had their patrons; they had their social connections, their cliques, and they looked at me as if I didn't exist. I was an outsider; I wasn't a member of their club. Invitations to read for parts came less and less often; finally, they didn't come at all. I didn't let that bother me, though; I kept on writing letters, I kept on with my career. I wrote to theater directors; even to those who no longer were in the business. Who knows, maybe they could've gotten back into it. Nobody ever wrote back. Except one. A few years ago a major theater invited me to audition. It had been a long time. I went; I read the part of Juliet, what else? I finished the scene and didn't hear a word from out front. A long pause. Suddenly, I heard a young man's voice: "Please go to the business office and collect your check for your expenses." In the darkness I couldn't recognize who it was, and a spotlight made it impossible for me to see into the theater seats. But I could see that he stood next to the director, obviously his assistant. I went to the business office. The door to the waiting room was open. I heard laughter from behind the office door; it opened as soon as I came in. There were four women present. One sat behind a desk, the others stood around her. The rumor must've spread like wildfire that there was a woman, no longer young—or should I say, now, middle-aged—who read the part of Juliet. The women looked at me and smiled. I knew that, in their eyes, I was completely ridiculous. Even the secretary looked at me with that same look, and the mail-boy, too, it seemed to me then, could hardly suppress his laughter when I walked past him on my way out. That was the last time I set foot in a theater. I've remained true to my art, true to my Juliet; I've learned no other role and am content to concentrate on Juliet, improving my grasp of the part, day by day, year by year. I used to work as a secretary at the Society for the Blind in order to pay for my acting lessons. But what good is an acting teacher who's constantly badgering me to learn other parts? No one understood me, not even the blind. Blind people are suspicious folks; they're always afraid that someone is going to take something from them.

I'm not going to take anything from anybody; I want to give them something. My art. My Juliet. What are you supposed to do if you don't have any money? Well, you do a lot of things. A few months ago I went to this fancy artist hangout downtown. All the big actors in town were there, self-satisfied and smug. They talked about the great successes they had and the great failures others had; they didn't notice that I was one of them, more than they could ever suppose. For thirty years, working every day, I had perfected Juliet. It was a piece of work never before seen on any stage in any town. A few tables away from me a director I recognized from his picture in the newspapers sat talking with friends. I kept staring at him until I caught his eye. I began to move my lips, doing Juliet, but not making a sound. He was fascinated, and I began to whisper the words. From across the room I whispered Juliet. Then, suddenly, he turned his back on me. Just like that, he turned his back on me. He was my last chance.

(*She regards the blind man—imploringly.*)

JASMINE: You are my last chance.

(*Silence. Very carefully, she removes his glasses. The pupilless whites of his eyes are visible. She moves her hand back and forth in front of his eyes. The eyes are sightless—lifeless. She looks at him and moves her lips without making a sound. The stage is completely silent. Slowly, very quietly, the first words of Juliet become audible. She is playing Juliet for him, her Juliet. She plays the part exceptionally well.*)

JASMINE:

    . . . but farewell compliment.
Dost thou love me? I know thou wilt say "Ay,"
And I will take thy word. Yet if thou swear'st
Thou mayst prove false. At lovers' perjuries,
They say, Jove laughs. O gentle Romeo,
If thou dost love, pronounce it faithfully.
Or if thou thinkest I am too quickly won,
I'll frown and be perverse and say thee nay,
So thou wilt woo, but else not for the world.
In truth, fair Montague, I am too fond,
And therefore thou mayst think my havior
    light.
But trust me, gentleman, I'll prove more true
Than those that have more coying to be
    strange.
I should have been more strange, I must con-
    fess,
But that thou overheardst, ere I was ware,
My true-love passion. Therefore pardon me,
And not impute this yielding to light love,
Which the dark night hath so discovered.

(*Silence. The rain beats against the window panes. Long silence.*)

55

JASMINE: Would you have taken me?

(*Silence.*)

BLIND MAN: Yes.

(*Jasmine stands in front of the blind man. She covers her face with her hands. The rain stops. Long silence.*)

BLIND MAN: You know who I am?

(*Jasmine places her face in his hands.*)

JASMINE: In your file at the Society for the Blind under the heading, "profession," beside travel guide, dish-washer and journalist, there was also—theater director. I didn't know what to make of it. Then I found your name in an old theater almanac. After the war you were the director of a small-town repertory theater.

BLIND MAN: I did manage three separate companies, nevertheless.

(*The blind man laughs. During the following dialogue, both break into occasional fits of laughter.*)

BLIND MAN: Theater, opera, ballet.

JASMINE: You were the last one I could have auditioned with.

BLIND MAN: If my eyesight hadn't degenerated so quickly, I would've been able to get a bigger theater in a bigger town.

JASMINE: I read in a trade paper that you were director for only a little while. There were some problems with your resume.

BLIND MAN: That's right. I didn't mention my Nazi past.

JASMINE: No, that wasn't it. You invented the bit about your stay in America and your directing experience on Broadway.

BLIND MAN: Is that right? It's been so long ago.

(*The two embrace. The blind man caresses Jasmine.*)

JASMINE: Do you realize just who it is you have in your arms?

BLIND MAN (*tenderly*): An absolutely crazy woman, fifty years old or so, with a rather unremarkable figure; a complete failure as an actress.

(*Silence.*)

BLIND MAN: And you? Do you have any idea who it is you have in your arms?

JASMINE (*tenderly*): Yes, I do. An old man. Still fooling himself, blind and impotent.

(*Silence. Jasmine and the blind man embrace tightly. Long silence. Their embrace loosens. The blind man goes into the next room. Jasmine opens a window, sits down on the camp cot and looks at the sky. Stars shine in the firmament. The blind man returns with a small radio, vintage 1956. He sits down on the cot and turns the radio on. He pushes a button. No sound. Jasmine takes the radio and turns the knobs. No sound. She looks to see what the matter is; there are no batteries in the radio. She places the radio next to the cot. The two look out at the heavens. It is completely quiet and still.)*

13.

(*Silence.*)

JASMINE: When was the first time you ran out of batteries?

(*Silence.*)

JASMINE: When you don't know what's going on the world, at least you're free to invent your own news, aren't you? You know, I'm pretty good at making things up.

BLIND MAN: The first time I ran out was from early 1962 to the middle of 1964.

JASMINE: Do you know what happened during that time?

BLIND MAN: I think that was about the time of the Cuban Missile Crisis, wasn't it? Or was that later?

JASMINE: Not at all. That's when we first met. I

auditioned for you. You listened to me throughout the whole thing. You didn't say a word. The hall was completely quiet. I moved forward, to the foot of the stage. Silence. I summoned all the courage left inside me. "Was it all right?" I asked. And suddenly, you said one sentence, one single sentence. "Go to the office and tell my assistant that you've got the part." I could've hugged you if the stage had not been so high.

(*Silence.*)

JASMINE: And the next time. When was the next time your batteries ran out.

BLIND MAN: 1968.

JASMINE: Oh yes, 1968. In the meantime you had just taken over a large theater. You produced Schiller's *Robbers*. I played Amalia. And the robber band was played by a bunch of long-haired students, young kids, really; some of them not even actors at all, just students. It was a real mess. And, to make matters worse, you and I had two different ideas of my role. We argued; we reconciled. It was fantastic. But, the reviews were mixed. So, what about the next time?

BLIND MAN: Wait, now, let me see. 1975?

(*The sound of an approaching Moped is heard. The*

two on stage are so caught up in their game that they take no notice of it.)

JASMINE: Unfortunately, by that time, we no longer had our own theater. We'd put together an original work and took it on the road. You directed. I played all the parts. It lasted four hours. The reviews were devastating. We swore we'd never read another newspaper again. But I didn't keep my word. At night I went to the train station and bought a paper. And who did I see standing next to the kiosk reading the entertainment section? You. At first we were really surprised; then, we hugged each other and laughed.

BLIND MAN: The next time I lost track of things because I ran out of batteries was 1986, in June. I remember that exactly. When Chernobyl happened, I remember wondering if I should buy any batteries at all.

JASMINE: 1986. The largest and greatest theater in the country, the National Theater, had openings. It was only after the most bizarre intrigues in the business, a wild publicity campaign and even some political intervention from the highest levels that they finally offered you the position. You became the Director of the National Theater. We moved in immediately. You opened with *Romeo and Juliet* ; I played Juliet—an incredible gamble. Everyone who had ever smirked at me or dismissed my acting ability was sitting there in the audience. They waited for my defeat. I stood in the wings and thought, "I'm going to die of nervousness." I went out and spoke my first lines.

(*Silence.*)

JASMINE: What more is there to say, but that it was an unparalleled success.

(*Jasmine takes the blind man by the hand. They take their bows before the audience, several times. Silence. Quietly, the boy enters. He wears a leather jacket and carries a motorcycle helmet under his arm. With his other hand he carries a package. The two take no notice of him. Silence. Jasmine and the blind man continue to take their bows.*)

JASMINE: We're on Olympus.

BLIND MAN: We are the greatest. We are the world's best. We are the finest theater in the world.

(*Silence. Jasmine notices the boy. Immediately, she ceases bowing. She lets go of the blind man's hand and opens her luggage. The blind man still bows a couple of more times, then, he, too, stops.*)

BLIND MAN: What's going on here?

BOY: The lady said I was supposed to come pick her up. We're leaving.

(*Jasmine takes her fur coat out of her luggage; she*

puts it on. She places her red wig back onto her head. The blind man clings to Jasmine. She frees herself; first, gently, then, more forcefully.)

BLIND MAN: Jasmine, I'm pleading with you; I'm begging you. Stay with me. It hurts so much.

(*Jasmine closes her luggage and moves to the door. The blind man imitates a donkey's squeal. It echoes painfully across the stage.*)

BLIND MAN: Jasmine. The pain is real. No imitations this time.

(*The blind man crawls toward the door. He grabs onto the boy's legs.*)

BLIND MAN: Boy, stay with me. Please. I'll let you say whatever you want, whatever you feel like. Anything's okay. What would you like to say to me? Who's on fire? The sky's on fire? Really? You know I don't have any batteries. How should I know what's happening in the world. Have they shot Castro yet? Or, did they hang him? Have the Germans got a new wall—this time, one that goes around the whole country? Who's killing who? Are the Croats killing the Serbs, or is it the Serbs killing Croats? How about the Italians killing the Albanians? Or, the Iraqis killing the Kurds? Who's arrested whom? Has the junta got all the reformers in jail? Or, the reformers the junta? Or, has

62

everyone put down their guns and made up? So, what's new in the world?!

(The boy throws the package of batteries at the blind man. The batteries fall out of the package and lie scattered on the floor. The blind man kneels and looks for the batteries, feeling about the floor. Then, he stands and goes to the wall. He takes the tyrolean hat from off its hook; he stands approximately one meter away from the mirror, faces the wall and tries on the hat. A short while passes before he seems satisfied with how the hat sits on his head. He goes to Jasmine and the boy, stretches out his arms, expecting them to take him by the hand.)

BLIND MAN: I'm going with you.

(Jasmine and the boy do not move. The blind man stands there, still with out-stretched arms. Silence.)

BLIND MAN *(shouts)*: Don't leave me alone! I'll rot here! Any attempt to take even one step toward the valley would kill me! I could howl my lungs out up here, and those people in town would take it for my newest imitation.

(The boy puts on his motorcycle helmet. Jasmine stands, wavering, at the door.)

BLIND MAN: What're you going to do down there, Jasmine? Walk the streets until they can spit up your legs? Audition one last time? Go back to the Society for the Blind and be ignored for the rest of your life? Remember what you said? We're on Olympus up here.

63

You're right, Jasmine. We are on Olympus.
We are the Gods. The Gods of Theater. We
have to keep on playing. He jests at scars
that never felt a wound. Second Act, second
scene. Romeo enters.

But soft, what light through yonder window
breaks?
It is the east, and Juliet is the sun.
Arise, fair sun, and kill the envious moon . . .
It is my lady, O, it is my love!
O, that she knew she were!
She speaks, yet she says nothing.
What of that?
Her eye discourses; I will answer it.
I am too bold. 'Tis not to me she speaks.
Two of the fairest stars inall the heaven,
Having some business, do entreat her eyes
To twinkle in their spheres till they return.
What if her eyes were there, they in her head?
The brightness of her cheek would shame
those stars
As daylight doth a lamp; her eyes in heaven
Would through the airy region stream so
bright
That birds would sing and think it were not
night.
See how she leans her cheek upon her hand!
O, that I were a glove upon that hand,
That I might touch that cheek!

(*Jasmine watches the blind man play Romeo. She*

picks up the batteries and gives them back to the boy. The boy runs from the room. Jasmine and the blind man enact the most famous of all scenes: the balcony scene. He plays the scene with tyrolean hat, she with her red wig and fur coat. She plays better than she has ever played.)

JASMINE: Ay, me!

BLIND MAN:

> She speaks!
> O, speak again, bright angel !

JASMINE:

> O Romeo, Romeo, wherefore art thou Romeo?
> Deny thy father and refuse thy name!
> Or, if thou wilt not, be but sworn my love,
> And I'll no longer be a Capulet!

BLIND MAN (aside):

> Shall I hear more, or shall I speak at
> this?

JASMINE:

> 'Tis but thy name that is my enemy;
> Thou art thyself, though not a Montague.
> What's Montague? . . .
> What's in a name? That which we call a rose
> By any other word would smell as sweet;
> So Romeo would, were he not Romeo called,
> Retain that dear perfection which he owes

Without that title. Romeo, doff thy name,
And for thy name, which is no part of thee,
Take all myself.

BLIND MAN (*while moving closer*):

I take thee at thy word!
Call me but love, and I'll be new baptized;
Henceforth I never will be Romeo.

JASMINE:

What art thou that, thus bescreened in night,
So stumblest on my counsel ?

BLIND MAN:

By a name
I know not how to tell thee who I am.

JASMINE:

My ears have not yet drunk a hundred words
Of thy tongue's uttering, yet I know the
sound:
Art thou not Romeo and a Montague?

BLIND MAN:

Neither, fair maid, if either thee dislike.

JASMINE:

How camest thou hither, tell me, and where
fore?

The orchard walls are high and hard to climb,
And the place death, considering who thou
art,
If any of my kinsmen find thee here.

BLIND MAN:

With love's light wings did I o'erperch
these walls,
For stony limits cannot hold love out,
And what love can do, that dares love
attempt;
Therefore thy kinsmen are no stop to me.

JASMINE:

Thou knowest the mask of night is on my face,
Else would a maiden blush bepaint my cheek
For that which thou hast heard me speak to
night.
Fain would I dwell on form—fain, fain deny
What I have spoke; but farewell compliment!
Dost thou love me?

BLIND MAN:

Lady, by yonder blessed moon I vow,
That tips with silver all these fruit-tree tops—

JASMINE:

O, swear not by the moon, th' inconstant
moon,
That monthly changes in her circled orb,

Lest that thy love prove likewise variable.

BLIND MAN:

What shall I swear by?

JASMINE:

Well, do not swear. Although I joy in thee,
I have no joy of this contract tonight.
It is too rash, too unadvised, too sudden,
Too like the lightning, which doth cease to be
Ere one can say 'It lightens.' Sweet, good
night!
This bud of love, by summer's ripening
breath,
May prove a beauteous flower when next we
meet.
Good night, good night!

BLIND MAN:

O, wilt thou leave me so unsatisfied?

JASMINE:

What satisfaction canst thou have tonight?

BLIND MAN: Th' exchange of thy love's faithful
vow for mine.

JASMINE:

I gave thee mine before thou didst request it;
. . . My bounty is as boundless as the sea,
My love as deep; the more I give to thee,

The more I have, for both are infinite.

BLIND MAN:

O blessed, blessed night! I am afeard,
Being in night, all this is but a dream,
Too flattering-sweet to be substantial.

*(The sound of an approaching moped is heard; the
sound grows louder. Jasmine breaks off the play
and runs to the open window. The boy comes down
the road at full throttle. It seems to be only a matter
of seconds before he crashes into a tree or outcrop-
ping of rocks. Jasmine screams in alarm and,
panic-ridden, closes the window. Silence. The blind
man moves slowly toward the window; he opens it.
Outside, there is no sound; only, the reflection of a
fiery wreckage rages up between the rocks. A small
alpine glow. Silence. The blind man turns away
from the window, looks out toward the audience,
tilts his head and smiles.)*

BLIND MAN: Dark and quiet, as usual.

ARIADNE PRESS

Studies in Austrian Literature, Culture and Thought

Major Figures of
Modern Austrian Literature
Edited by Donald G. Daviau

Major Figures of
Turn-of-the-Century
Austrian Literature
Edited by Donald G. Daviau

Austrian Writers and the
Anschluss: Understanding the
Past—Overcoming the Past
Edited by Donald G. Daviau

Introducing Austria
A Short History
By Lonnie Johnson

The Verbal and Visual Art of
Alfred Kubin
By Phillip H. Rhein

Austria in the Thirties
Culture and Politics
Edited by Kenneth Segar
and John Warren

Kafka and Language: In the
Stream of Thoughts and Life
By G. von Natzmer Cooper

Robert Musil and the Tradition
of the German Novelle
By Kathleen O'Connor

Blind Reflections:
Gender in Elias Canetti's
Die Blendung
By Kristie A. Foell

Coexistent Contradictions
Joseph Roth in Retrospect
Edited by Helen Chambers

Stefan Zweig:
An International Bibliography
By Randolph J. Klawiter

Implied Dramaturgy:
Robert Musil and the Crisis
of Modern Drama
By Christian Rogowski

Quietude and Quest
Protagonists and Antagonists in
the Theater, on and off Stage
As Seen Through the Eyes of
Leon Askin
By Leon Askin and C.M. Davidson

"What People Call Pessimism":
Sigmund Freud, Arthur Schnitzler
and Nineteenth-Century
Controversy at the University
of Vienna Medical School
By Mark Luprecht

Arthur Schnitzler and Politics
By Adrian Clive Roberts

Structures of Disintegration:
Narrative Strategies in
Elias Canetti's Die Blendung
By David Darby

Of Reason and Love:
The Life and Works of Marie
von Ebner-Eschenbach
By Carl Steiner

ARIADNE PRESS
New Titles

Lerida
By Alexander Giese
Translation and Afterword
by Lowell A. Bangerter

Charade
By Friedrich Ch. Zauner
Translation and Afterword
by Michael Roloff

Three Flute Notes
By Jeannie Ebner
Translation and Afterword
by Lowell A. Bangerter

Siberia and Other Plays
By Felix Mitterer

The Sphere of Glass
By Marianne Gruber
Translation and Afterword
by Alexandra Strelka

The Convent School
By Barbara Frischmuth
Translated by
G. Chapple and J.B. Lawson

The Green Face
By Gustav Meyrink
Translated by Michael Mitchell

*The Ariadne Book of Austrian
Fantasy: The Meyrink Years
1890-1930*
Ed. & trans. by Michael Mitchell

Try Your Luck!
By Peter Rosei
Translated by Kathleen Thorpe

Walpurgisnacht
By Gustav Meyrink
Translated by Michael Mitchell

The Cassowary
By Matthias Mander
Translation and Afterword
by Michael Mitchell

Plague in Siena
By Erich Wolfgang Skwara
Foreword by Joseph P. Strelka
Translation by Michael Roloff

Memories with Trees
By Ilse Tielsch
Translation and Afterword
by David Scrase

Aphorisms
By Marie von Ebner-Eschenbach
Translated by David Scrase and
Wolfgang Mieder

Conversations with Peter Rosei
By Wilhelm Schwarz
Translated by C. & T. Tessier

*Anthology of Contemporary
Austrian Folk Plays*
By V. Canetti, Preses/Becher,
Mitterer, Szyszkowitz, Turrini
Translation and Afterword
by Richard Dixon

The Calm Ocean
By Gerhard Roth
Translated by
Helga Schreckenberger and
Jacqueline Vansant

ARIADNE PRESS

Translation Series: